Brain Busters™ II

picture puzzles to sharpen
right-brain thinking and music knowledge

Created by

Brenda Knowis

Editor: Kris Kropff
Cover and Book design: Brenda Knowis

Printed in the
United States of America

ISBN: 0-00000-000-0

Permission to Reproduce Notice

HMP
HERITAGE MUSIC PRESS
A Division of The Lorenz Corporation
Box 802 / Dayton, OH 45401-0802
www.lorenz.com

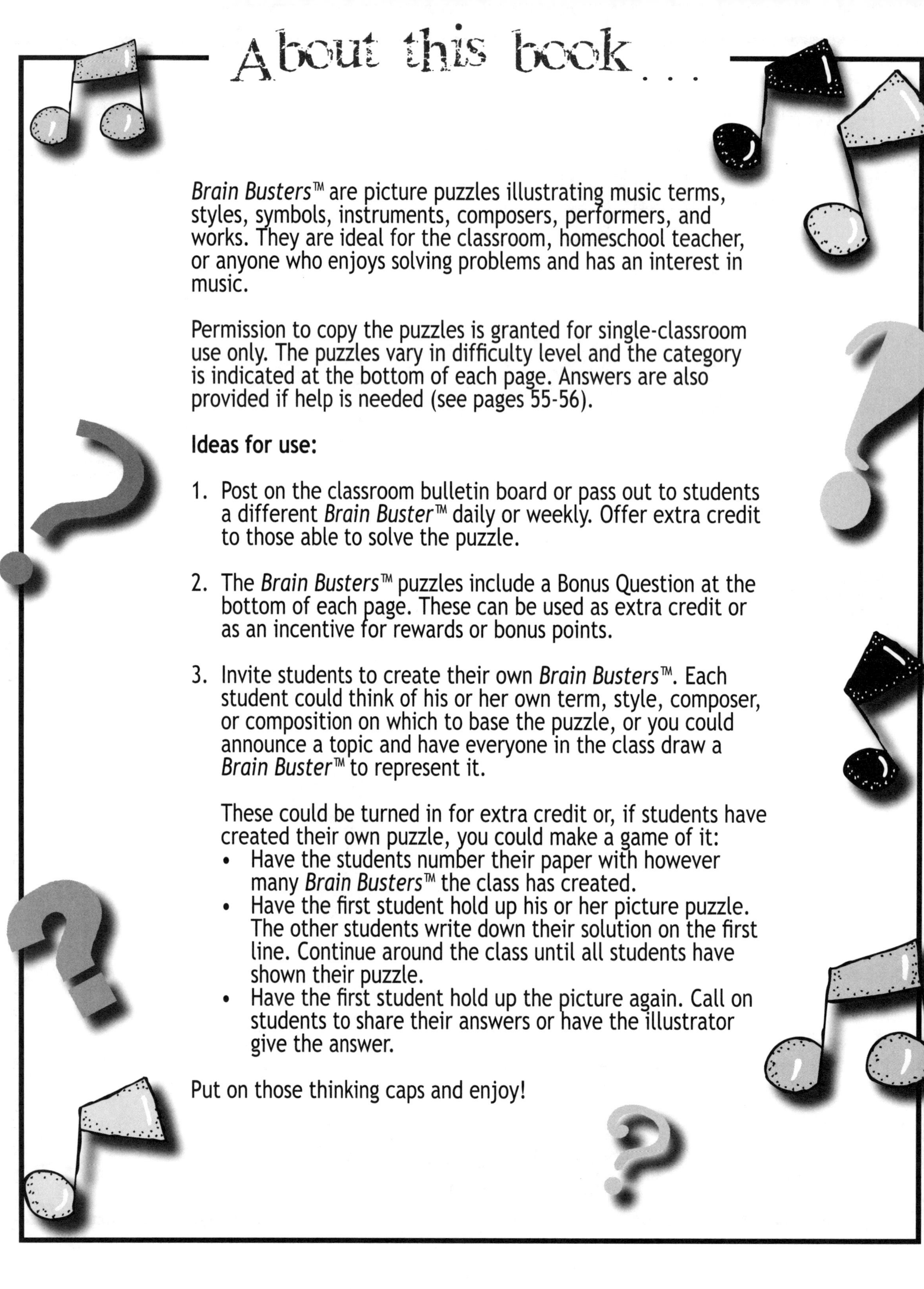

About this book...

Brain Busters™ are picture puzzles illustrating music terms, styles, symbols, instruments, composers, performers, and works. They are ideal for the classroom, homeschool teacher, or anyone who enjoys solving problems and has an interest in music.

Permission to copy the puzzles is granted for single-classroom use only. The puzzles vary in difficulty level and the category is indicated at the bottom of each page. Answers are also provided if help is needed (see pages 55-56).

Ideas for use:

1. Post on the classroom bulletin board or pass out to students a different *Brain Buster*™ daily or weekly. Offer extra credit to those able to solve the puzzle.

2. The *Brain Busters*™ puzzles include a Bonus Question at the bottom of each page. These can be used as extra credit or as an incentive for rewards or bonus points.

3. Invite students to create their own *Brain Busters*™. Each student could think of his or her own term, style, composer, or composition on which to base the puzzle, or you could announce a topic and have everyone in the class draw a *Brain Buster*™ to represent it.

   These could be turned in for extra credit or, if students have created their own puzzle, you could make a game of it:
   - Have the students number their paper with however many *Brain Busters*™ the class has created.
   - Have the first student hold up his or her picture puzzle. The other students write down their solution on the first line. Continue around the class until all students have shown their puzzle.
   - Have the first student hold up the picture again. Call on students to share their answers or have the illustrator give the answer.

Put on those thinking caps and enjoy!

Bonus Question: Who wrote this piece? _______________________________

Category: Composition

Brain Busters II

Bonus Question: What is the definition of this term? _______________________

____

O

+

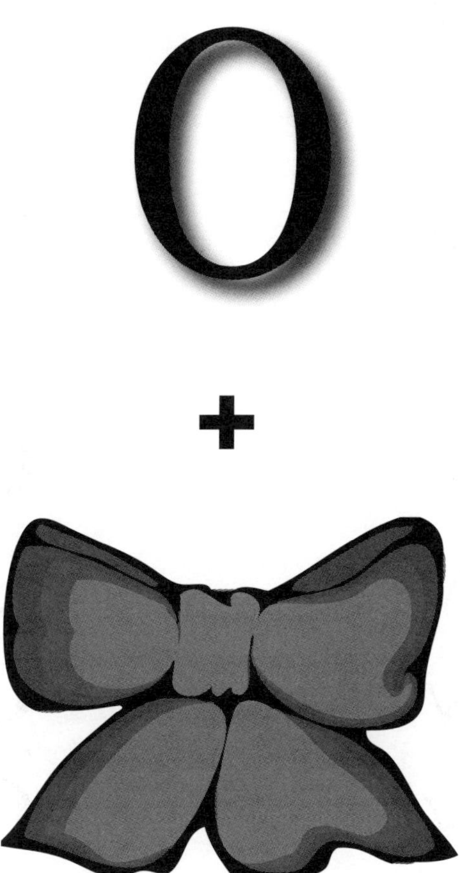

Bonus Question: This instrument is a member of which family? _______________________

Category: Instrument

Century	Century
Century	Century
Century	Century
Century	Century
Century	Century
Century	Century
Century	Century
Century	Century
Century	Century
Century	↗ Century

Bonus Question: Composers during this period experimented with new ways of making sounds, like putting nuts and washers on the strings in a piano.

True　　　　　　　　　　**False**

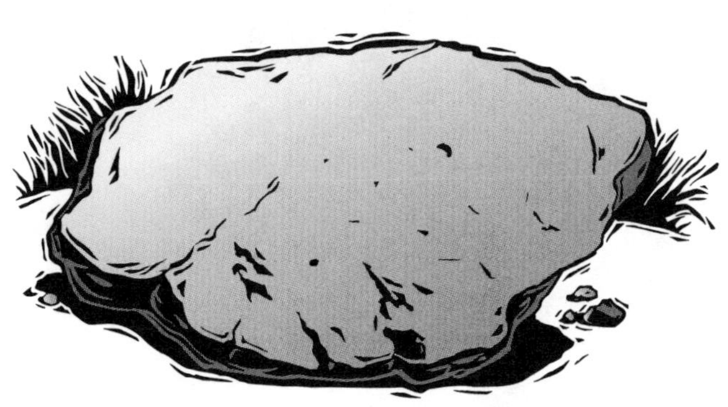

+

Bonus Question: He composed during the Baroque Period.

True   **False**

Category: Composer

Bonus Question: One of his most famous works is the opera, *Carmen*.

True   **False**

Category: Composer

A

+

+

+

Bonus Question: What folk dance is often accompanied by this instrument?

Category: Instrument

Brain Busters II

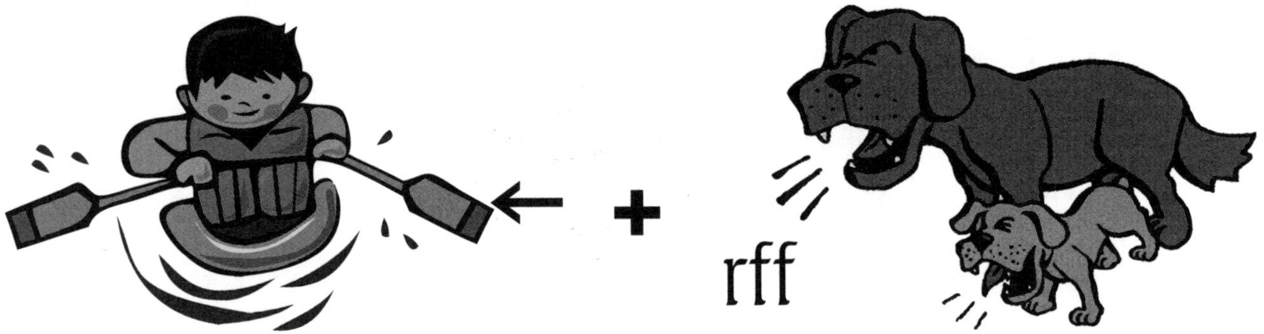

Bonus Question: This German composer developed an approach for teaching music in school.

          True   False

Category: Composer

+

+

T

Bonus Question: He wrote over 600 songs.

True   False

Category: Composer

+

IH

+

Bonus Question: Circle the words below that best describe this style.

Elegant   Dissonant

Simple   Emotional

Category: Style

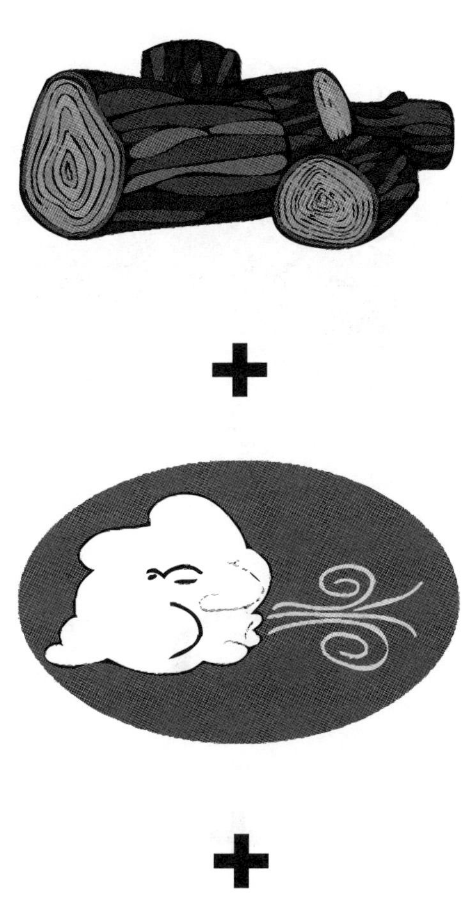

+

+

S

Bonus Question: Circle the instruments from the list below that belong to this family.

Trombone	Flute	Oboe
Saxophone	Snare Drum	Violin
Bassoon	Tambourine	Clarinet

Category: Instrument Family

\+

O

\+

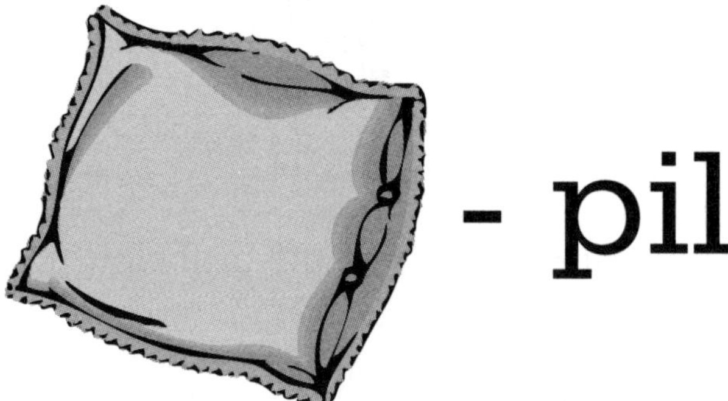

- pil

Bonus Question: This instrument is a member of what family?

Brain Busters II

ERIC

Bonus Question: What instrument does this person play?

Category: Artist/Performer

+

BOP

Bonus Question: When was this style of jazz developed?

1980s-90s   1940s-50s   1890s-1900s

Category: Style

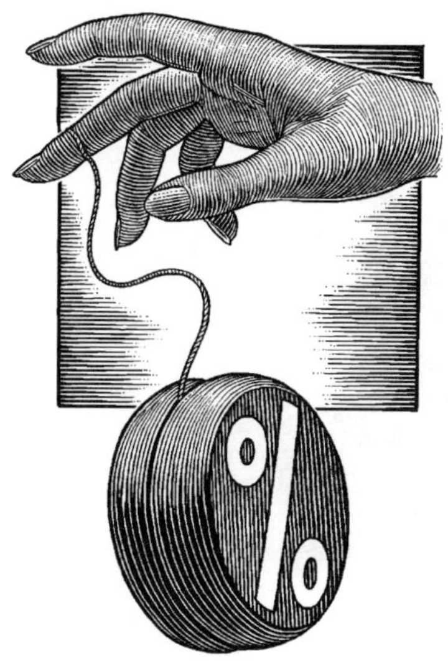

Bonus Question: What instrument does this musician play? ___________________________

Category: Artist/Performer

Brain Busters II

- char

+

Bonus Question: Circle the instrument this jazz musician played.

Piano   Drums   Trumpet   Saxophone

Brain Busters II

+

Bonus Question: Circle the musician below that sings in this style.

LL Cool J   Johnny Cash   Britney Spears

                    Category: Style

Bonus Question: Who wrote this famous ballet? _______________________

Brain Busters II

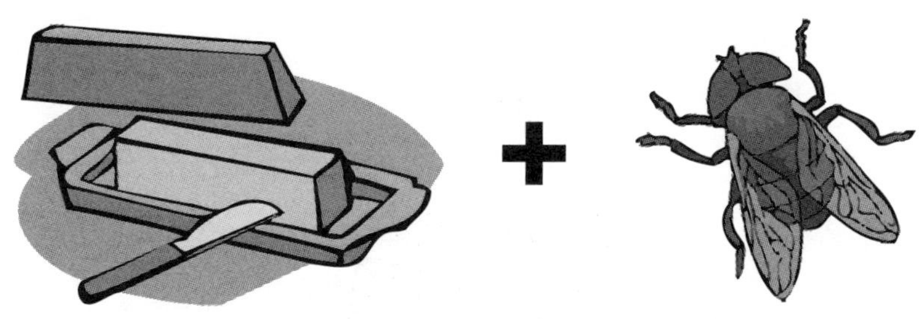

Bonus Question: Who wrote this famous opera?

Category: Composition

+

Z

+

Bonus Question: Music by this composer best fits in which of these styles?

Romantic   Classical   Baroque

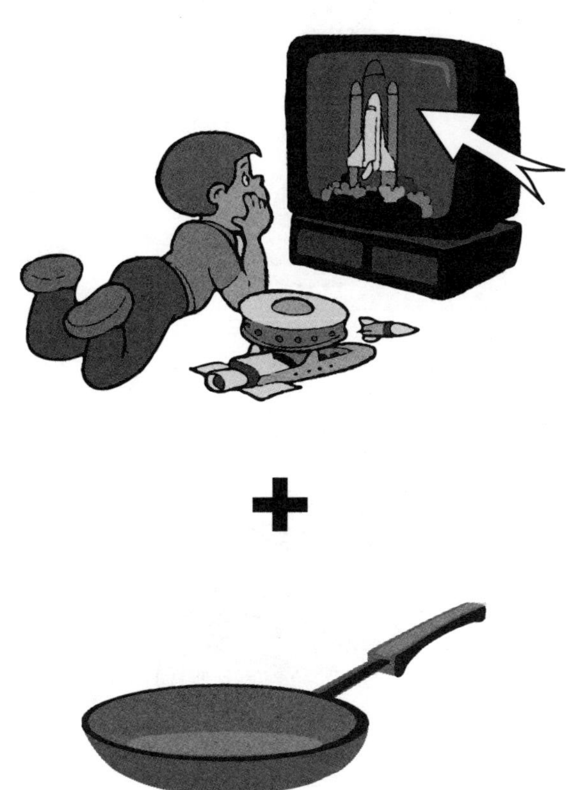

+

Bonus Question: Circle the style from the list below that best describes his music.

Romantic   Classical   Baroque

Category: Composer

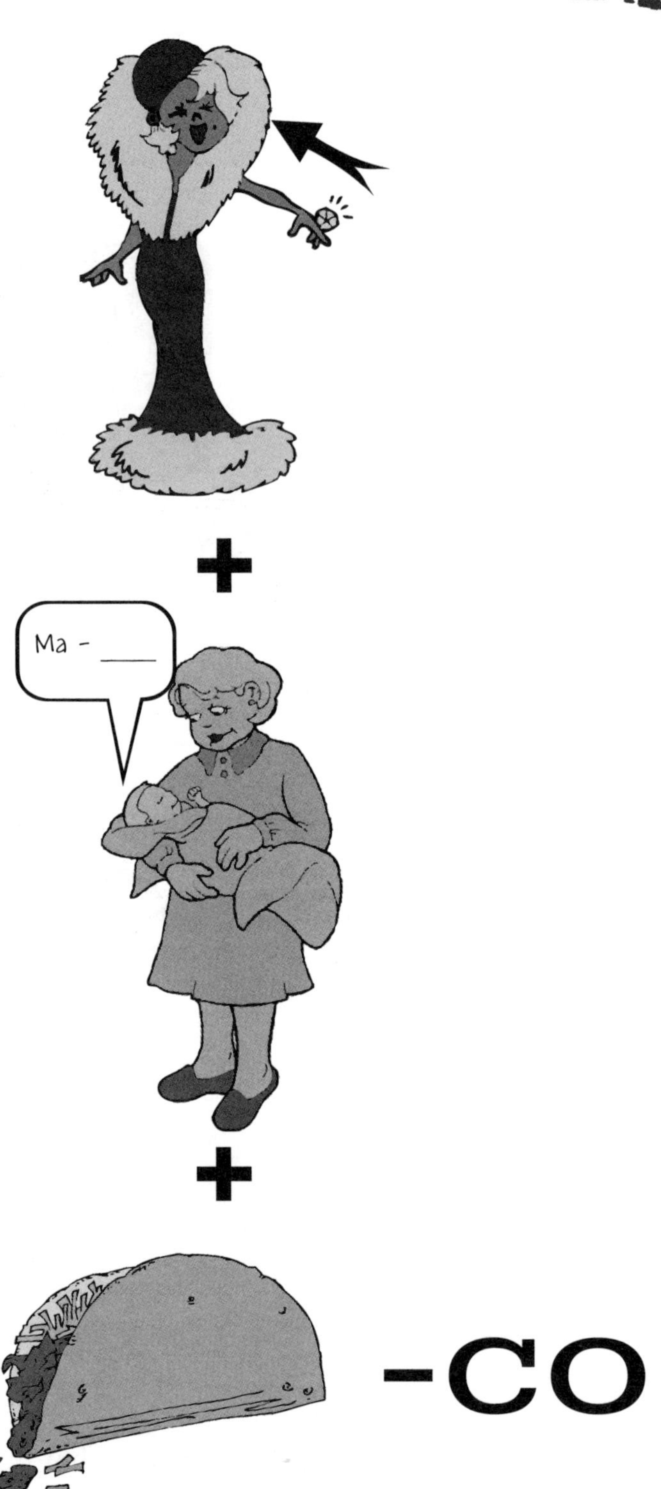

-CO

Bonus Question: Circle the symbol that represents this term.

>   ⊕   *p*   ⌢   ♩♩   *mp*

 .  . 

Bonus Question: This guitarist is known for playing
what style of music? _______________________

25

SYMPHO

Bonus Question: Who composed this piece? ______________________________

Brain Busters II

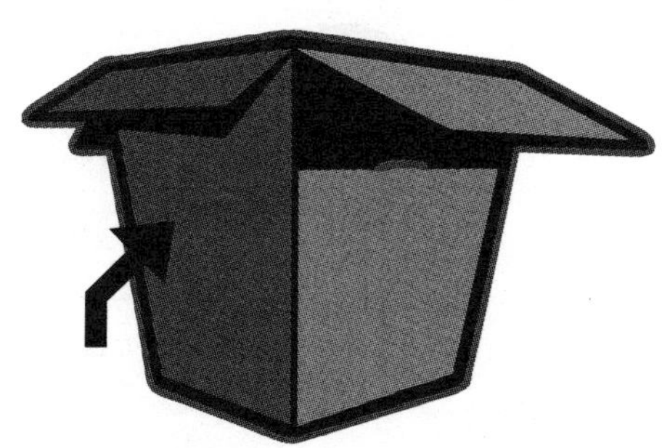

Bonus Question: Who wrote this famous musical?______________________________________

Category: Composition

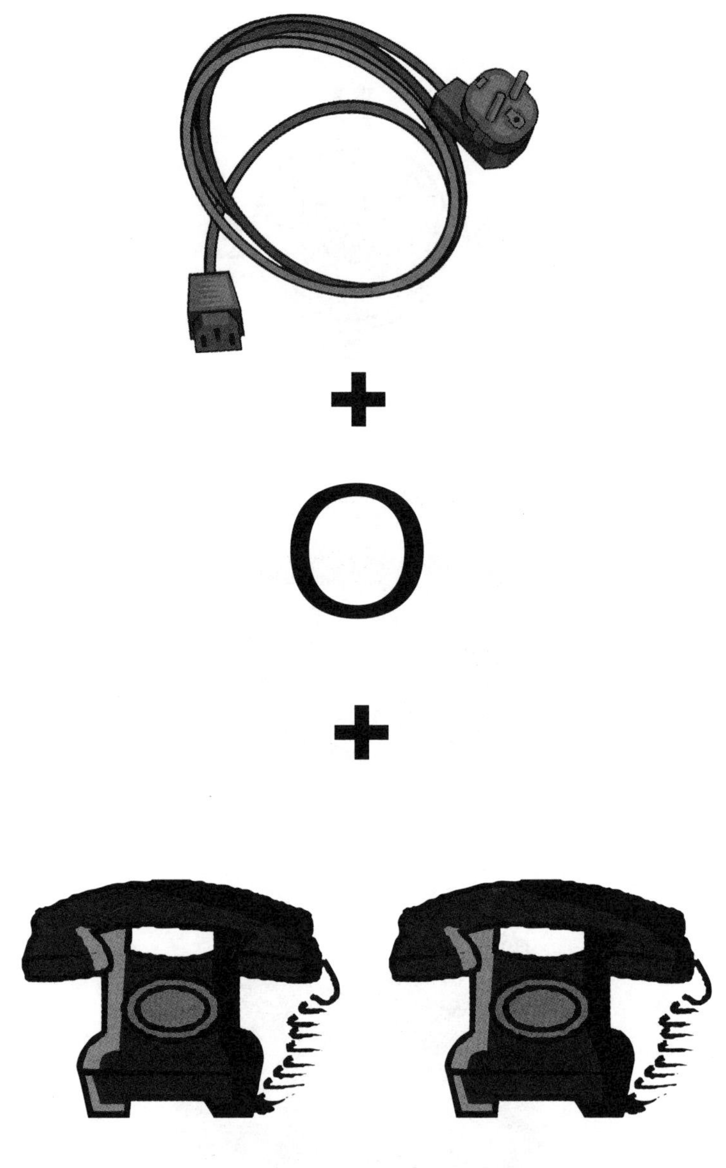

Bonus Question: Circle the instrument(s) below that are part of this family, which all produce sound through the vibration of strings.

Harp	Flute	Cello	Tuba	Vibraphone	Piano
Oboe	Guitar	Violin	Trumpet	String Bass	Cymbals

Category: Instrument Classification

+

AH

+

Bonus Question: What is the definition of this term?

____

Category: Term

FIDDLER ROOF

Bonus Question: This musical won 9 Tony Awards, including best musical, composer and lyricist.

True   False

Category: Composition

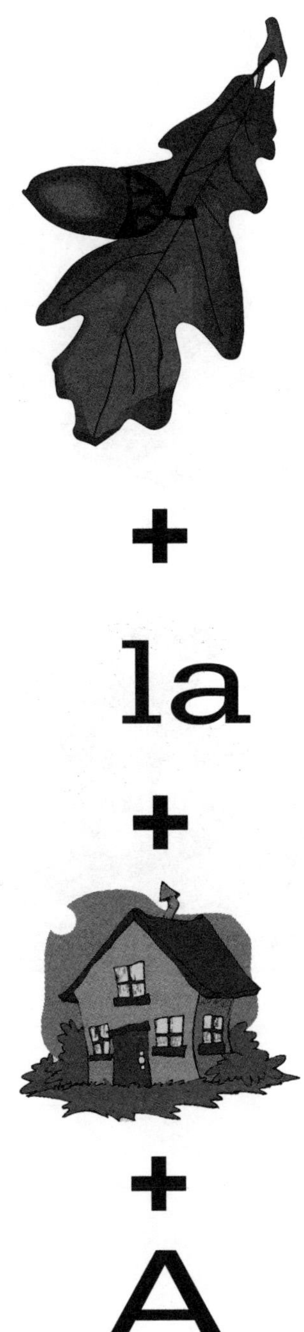

Bonus Question: Who wrote the music for this famous show?

____

Category: Composition

Bonus Question: This was Broadway's first large-scale epic drama, so large that it set a record for the number of performers in the cast. Circle the number of people you think were in the cast.

42　　　　96　　　　127

Category: Composition

VALLEY

Bonus Question: This piece is an example of what style of music? Circle the correct answer from the list below.

Bluegrass　　　　New Age　　　Gospel　　　　Swing

　　Reggae　　　Blues　　　Dixieland　　　　Boogie-Woogie

　　　　　　　　Bebop　　　　　　Salsa

Category: Composition

+

+

IN

Bonus Question: This instrument, often heard in bluegrass music, is a member of what family?

____

Category: Instrument

Brain Busters II

BAND

Bonus Question: Many people enjoy dancing to this style of jazz, which first became popular in the 1940s. Circle the person below who is NOT a famous big band leader.

Count Basie

Glenn Miller

Harry Connick, Jr.

Miles Davis

Category: Style

Bonus Question: During which period did this composer write?

____

Category: Composer

A

+

+

Bonus Question: What is the definition of this term?

Category: Term

+

Bonus Question: Circle the country where this composer was born.

America   Germany   Italy

Category: Composer

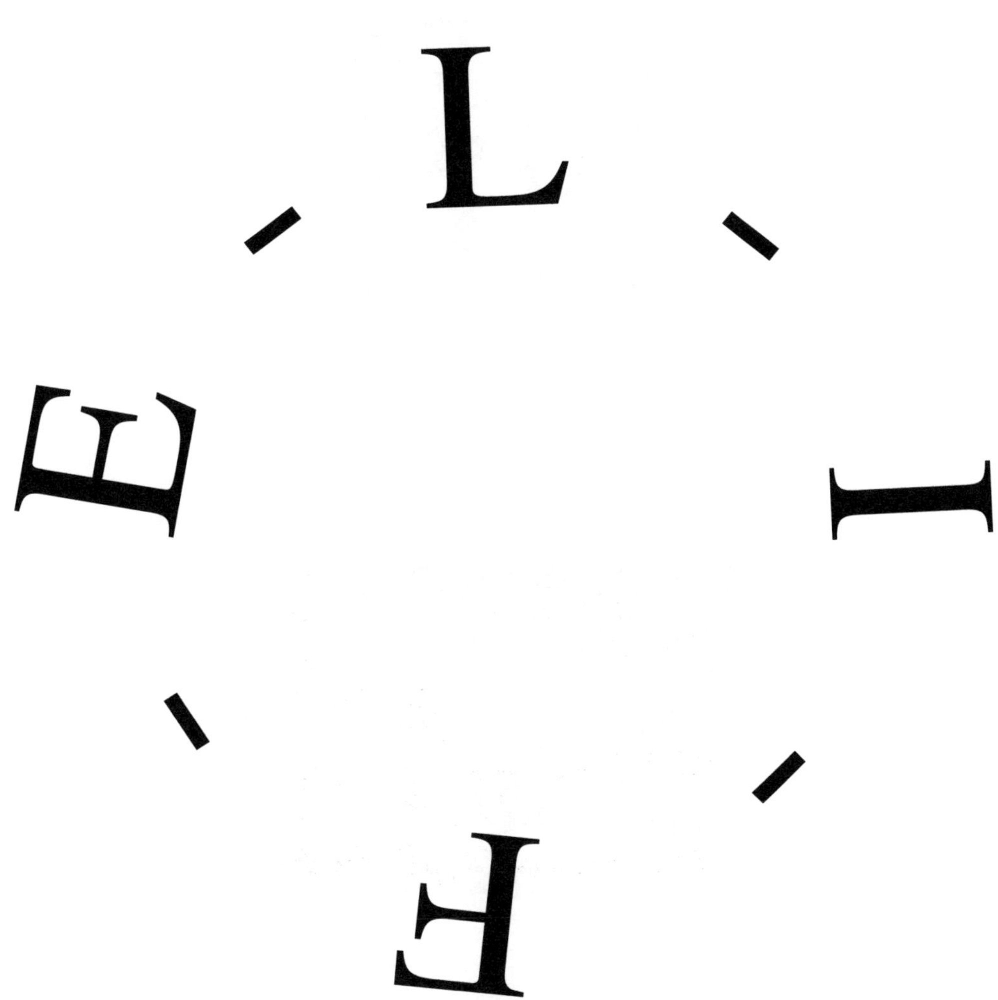

Bonus Question: This song is from a movie that was also made into a Broadway musical. Name that movie/musical.

Category: Composition

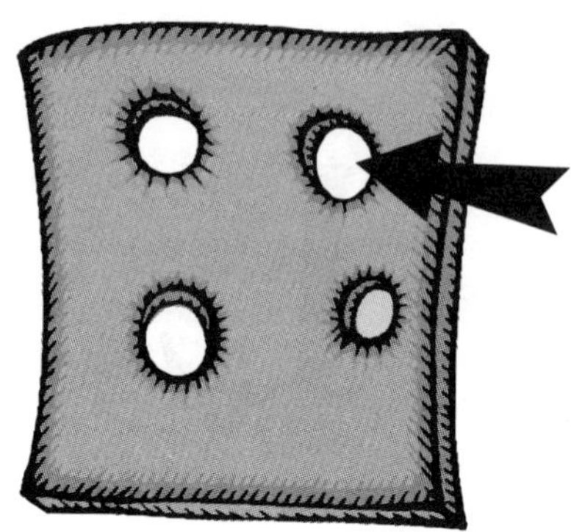

Bonus Question: How many beats does this receive in $\frac{4}{4}$ time?

+

Bonus Question: What does this term mean?

Category: Term

Bonus Question: How many beats does this receive?

MAJOR

Bonus Question: This is a series of how many notes?

3   12   8

Category: Term

Metro

+

Bonus Question: Do you know what this is used for? Write a brief description below.

pro & ____

+

+

- nado

Bonus Question: This term is the name for the person who leads a large musical ensemble, like a band or orchestra.

True   False

Category: Term

+

Bonus Question: This term means the adding or repeating of a piece due to overwhelming enthusiasm from the audience. True or false, it usually occurs at the beginning of a concert.

True   **False**

Category: Term

Bonus Question: This instrument is a member of what instrument family?

____

Category: Instrument

Bonus Question: This is a ceremonial prelude or flourish commonly played by brass instruments.

True   False

Category: Term

STEP

Bonus Question: How many of these are there in an octave? ________________

Category: Term

Bonus Question: Circle the decade when this instrument was invented.

1890s   1930s   1970s

Category: Instrument

Bonus Question: This famous piece is an example of what musical genre? Choose from the answers below.

Ballet   String Quartet   Symphony

Category: Composition

TROM

\+

Bonus Question: This instrument is in the brass family. Name another instrument in that family? ___________________________________

Bonus Question: Circle the country where this instrument originated.

America   Japan   Africa   India

Category: Instrument

Someone to Watch

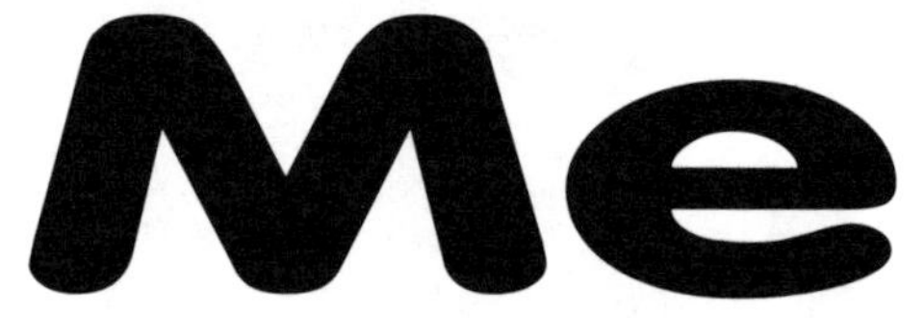

Bonus Question: This song has been perforned by Ella Fitzgerald, Frank Sinatra and countless others. Who wrote it? _______________________________

Answer Key

Page	Answer	Bonus Answer
3	Double Concerto in D Minor	J.S. Bach
4	Presto	Very Fast
5	Oboe	Woodwind
6	Twentieth Century	True
7	Rachmaninoff	False
8	Bizet	True
9	Accordian	Polka
10	Carl Orff	True
11	Schubert	True
12	Classical	Elegant; Simple
13	Woodwinds	Saxophone, Bassoon, Flute, Oboe, Clarinet
14	Piccolo	Woodwind
15	Eric Clapton	Guitar
16	Bebop	1940s-1950s
17	Yo-Yo Ma	Cello
18	Coltrane	Saxophone
19	Country	Johnny Cash
20	*Sleeping Beauty*	Tchaikovsky
21	*Madama Butterfly*	Puccini
22	Mozart	Classical
23	Chopin	Romantic
24	Fermata	𝄐
25	B.B. King	Blues
26	*Unfinished Symphony*	Schubert
27	*West Side Story*	Leonard Bernstein
28	Chordophones	Harp, Guitar, Cello, Violin, String Bass, Piano
29	Legato	To play or sing groups of notes smoothly
30	*Fiddler on the Roof*	True
31	*Oklahoma*	Richard Rogers
32	*Show Boat*	96

Answer Key

Page	Answer	Bonus Answer
33	Peace in the Valley	Gospel
34	Mandolin	String
35	Big Band Swing	Miles Davis
36	Mendelssohn	Romantic
37	Allegro	Cheerful, quick or fast
38	Bernstein	America
39	*Circle of Life*	*The Lion King*
40	Whole Rest	4
41	Molto	very
42	Quarter Rest	1
43	Major Scale	8
44	Metronome	An adjustable device that indicates the exact tempo of a piece.
45	Conductor	True
46	Encore	False
47	Violin	String
48	Fanfare	True
49	Half Step	12
50	Electric Piano	1930s
51	*Swan Lake*	Ballet
52	Trombone	Trumpet; F Horn; Tuba; Euphonium
53	Talking Drum	Africa
54	Someone to Watch Over Me	Gershwin